THE MANAGER'S TR POCKETBOOK

C000048669

By Ian Fleming
Drawings by Alan Roe

"Very user-friendly, informative and thought provoking. A must for managers involved in, or with, training."
Mary Douglas, Production Director, Seven Seas.

CONTENTS

INTRODUCTION

This book is for people responsible for ensuring that staff in organisations are trained.

You could be in a formal position, ie:

● management development/training manager, adviser, training officer or instructor.

Alternatively, training may simply be part of your job as a:

● manager, supervisor, departmental/section head, team leader or occasional presenter on courses.

Throughout the book you will come across specific advice for managers, indicated by the symbol $\boxed{M}$ *, and for trainers, indicated by the symbol* $\boxed{T}$ *.*

INTRODUCTION

WHY BOTHER TO TRAIN?

- After all, there are plenty of people on the job market (true, but how many have the skills and experience you need?).

- For a variety of reasons not every organisation trains its staff (again this is sadly true but things are changing .... people are increasingly coming to expect training as part of their job).

- Many organisations see training as an investment with a long term payoff— and they are not prepared to wait. So they buy in the skills needed.

- Unfortunately, in difficult circumstances some organisations put their investment of time, energies and money elsewhere and very often not in training.

REASONS FOR TRAINING
RESPONDING TO CHANGE

You need training to help your organisation survive in and respond to a changing world. Consider:

● both the pace and nature of change in our lives and organisations

● the demands and expectations of customers that often lead to:
  — greater customer focus
  — radical ways of operating
  — cost savings
  — greater flexibility of people in the workplace
  — changing shapes of organisations, fewer levels, broader jobs, reduced 'resources'
  — uncertainty about the future/reduced job security.

All these have implications for people's jobs and how they do them.

Successful organisations will be those who help their people respond to and meet the challenges surrounding change.

REASONS FOR TRAINING
RESPONDING TO BUSINESS NEEDS

If you are a trainer, how do you go about persuading higher management (a possibly sceptical audience) to invest in training?

Much has been written about the current need to:

- be customer focused
- provide quality products or services
- empower staff.

If this is the case in your organisation, then try pointing out that the key to delivering this is having staff who:

- know what's expected of them and why
- have the skills, confidence and support from above to deliver.

REASONS FOR TRAINING
IGNORANCE IS EXPENSIVE

The lack of trained staff could very well cost the organisation dearly, ie:

- mistakes and wasted materials/efforts
- demotivated staff
- high turnover

and more importantly . . . . .

- unhappy customers.

WHOSE JOB IS IT TO TRAIN?

Training and development are the responsibility of everyone in an organisation, not just those in formal training positions.

Starting at the top with the **chief executive/managing director** who:

- provides the vision of where the organisation needs to be
- sets an example in the form of leadership, and thereby ....
- creates within the organisation the desire to achieve.

Continuing with the **managers/supervisors** who are:

- closest to the staff (often in day to day contact)
- in a position to spot a need and influence performance.

It is also the responsibility of the **individual** to:

- take control of their own learning and manage their career.

TRAINING IN CONTEXT

Bear in mind:

- That training is going on all the time.

- The solving of everyday problems and situations is as much a part of the learning process as any training course.

- Training is not an end in itself; on its own it produces no business results. It needs to focus on and be responsive to organisational strategies, and make a contribution towards their achievement.

- Training is an investment but is also a cost.

- Its contribution to the business must be thought through.

TRAINING OR DEVELOPMENT?

In a changing world — where very little would appear to be secure — responsibility for developing skills and managing careers rests with the individual.

Nowadays the onus is shifting towards **SELF DEVELOPMENT**.

Against this background perhaps it is more relevant to talk about 'learning and development' than simply training and education. They say more about results than input and activity.

THE COSTS

Remember— Training isn't cheap. Before embarking on any training initiative, consider the costs of:

- **Your time**
  - to put it together and be involved
- **Participants**
  - the time they will spend attending
  - travel and possibly accommodation
  - arranging cover for their jobs whilst they are away
  - loss of business (opportunity costs)
- **Providing a venue**
  - hire of room and equipment (videos, computers, projectors)
  - food and refreshments
- **Speaker's time**
  - for example, consultants' fees and expenses
- **Getting it wrong**

(10) Management training often has a higher unit cost than any other type of training.

RECOGNISING TRAINING NEEDS

THE NEED FOR ACCURACY

Accurately identifying needs is the first step in putting together any training and learning initiative.

Carried out properly it will increase the chances of:

- putting together appropriate help where necessary
- measuring the impact of any help on performance and business objectives.

Time, effort and money are very often wasted if the needs have been poorly diagnosed. So ask yourself:

- what do people **NEED** in order to do their job in a different way and/or with more confidence?

Note: Not all 'needs' can be met by training. Some may need a change in the way that the business is run or a fresh look at any policies in place.

(12)

RECOGNISING TRAINING NEEDS

PLACES TO LOOK

Training needs can arise in many ways:

- through the setting of objectives
- from appraisals and reviews of performance
- as a result of mistakes being made
- from poor performance, ie: failure to reach standard
- observing people in action
- individuals asking for help
- customer complaints
- the time taken to do a job
- changes in: — legislation
  - work methods, systems, procedures
  - job content and responsibilities.

WILL IT ADD VALUE?

- Resources, ie: people's time and your money, are too valuable to waste, so only train if you have to.

- Training should be measured against the benefits to the organisation, ie: if we develop people's skills how will it add value to the business?

- Remember to consider non-training alternatives (where appropriate), eg:
  — making changes to the systems
  — re-designing the jobs that people do.

NEEDS IDENTIFICATION

In simple terms, needs can be identified on the following levels:

RECOGNISING TRAINING NEEDS

QUESTIONNAIRE

Consider the following as a guide to identifying needs and add your own examples where necessary.

Ask yourself what needs you have in your organisation (or department) under the following headings:

CUSTOMERS

How much have you a need to:

Rate the importance of each item on a scale ranging from 1 (low) to 10 (high)

- Improve the quality of your products
- Introduce new products/services
- Attract new customers
- Improve customer service
- Retain existing customers
- ....
- ....
- ....

RECOGNISING TRAINING NEEDS

QUESTIONNAIRE

FINANCIAL

Rate the importance of each
item on a scale ranging
from 1 (low) to 10 (high)

- Improve overall profitability
- Reduce costs
- Improve cash flow
- Make better use of financial data
- Improve financial/business planning
- Budget for future activities
- . . . .
- . . . .
- . . . .

RECOGNISING TRAINING NEEDS

QUESTIONNAIRE

PEOPLE

Rate the importance of each item on a scale ranging from 1 (low) to 10 (high)

- Reduce turnover
- Improve morale
- Increase the skills and confidence of staff
- Redesign jobs
- Encourage job flexibility
- Improve communications at all levels
- Introduce manpower and succession planning
- . . . .
- . . . .
- . . . .

RECOGNISING TRAINING NEEDS

QUESTIONNAIRE

LEGISLATION

Rate the importance of each item on a scale ranging from 1 (low) to 10 (high)

- Ensure that current legislation is complied with   _____
- Plan for the introduction of new legislation   _____
- . . . .   _____
- . . . .   _____
- . . . .   _____

OTHER AREAS

- Need to move premises   _____
- Introduction/development of IT systems   _____
- . . . .   _____

RECOGNISING TRAINING NEEDS

QUESTIONNAIRE
ANALYSIS

Now note the 5 items that you have scored the highest.

1 . . . .
2 . . . .
3 . . . .
4 . . . .
5 . . . .

- Ask yourself whether acquiring knowledge and skills will help these needs?

- If you answer 'yes' to any then you have a potential training need.

- If the answer is 'no' you may have to find ways of meeting the need other than training.

Adapted from Tad Leduchowicz writing in *'Improving Trainer Effectiveness'* pub. Gower.

RECOGNISING TRAINING NEEDS

ASSESSING PERFORMANCE

$\boxed{M}$ An important, yet often difficult, task of any manager is to analyse the performance of their staff, eg:

- if people are not performing to the standard expected of them, then why is this?

- in what areas do staff need to improve?

- is training or some other action the answer to performance improvement?

The next few pages contain a practical way of identifying the action that can be taken to improve performance.

ASSESSING PERFORMANCE

You have potentially a lot of data with which to gauge a person's performance.

● Look at the job description to identify the areas of skills, knowledge and experience required to do the job satisfactorily.

● Consider any objectives that have been set for the individual.

● In which of the above areas is the individual not performing adequately?

● Are any of these shortfalls caused by the fact that they lack skills, knowledge and/or experience?

If the answer is 'yes' then action such as appropriate training, coaching or job rotation needs to be taken.

If it is 'no' then other action needs to be taken such as that outlined in the Performance Flowchart.

RECOGNISING TRAINING NEEDS

PERFORMANCE FLOWCHART

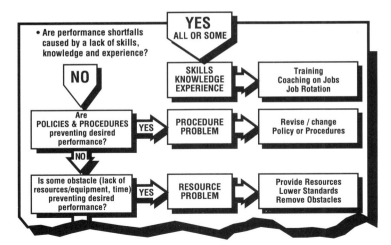

- Are performance shortfalls caused by a lack of skills, knowledge and experience?

YES ALL OR SOME

NO

	SKILLS KNOWLEDGE EXPERIENCE	Training Coaching on Jobs Job Rotation

Are POLICIES & PROCEDURES preventing desired performance?

YES → PROCEDURE PROBLEM → Revise / change Policy or Procedures

NO

Is some obstacle (lack of resources/equipment, time) preventing desired performance?

YES → RESOURCE PROBLEM → Provide Resources Lower Standards Remove Obstacles

23

PERFORMANCE FLOWCHART

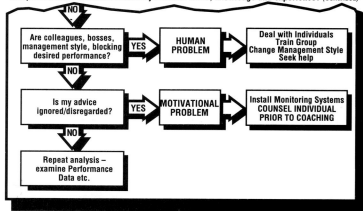

• Are performance shortfalls caused by a lack of skills, knowledge and experience? *(Continued)*

NO

| Are colleagues, bosses, management style, blocking desired performance? | **YES** | **HUMAN PROBLEM** | Deal with Individuals Train Group Change Management Style Seek help |

NO

| Is my advice ignored/disregarded? | **YES** | **MOTIVATIONAL PROBLEM** | Install Monitoring Systems COUNSEL INDIVIDUAL PRIOR TO COACHING |

NO

| Repeat analysis – examine Performance Data etc. |

With thanks to Interaction Training

24

RECOGNISING TRAINING NEEDS

AVOID GENERALISATION

'Financial awareness, managing staff and improving communications skills' are all descriptions too broad to be of help to anyone.

Consider what skills might be involved in each.

- Financial awareness could include:
  — the ability to put together a budget for a department
  — understanding the breakdown of costs and their application to an individual's department
  — being able to read, understand and use financial data/information.

- Managing staff might involve:
  — recognising the talents and abilities of their staff
  — setting objectives for both groups and individuals
  — maintaining team spirit whilst under pressure.

AVOID GENERALISATION

Communication skills could call for the ability to:

— present information both formally and informally to groups

— 'sell' decisions of others to their own staff

— accurately listen to the views of others and, where appropriate, feed them back to selected individuals.

All three areas are open to a variety of interpretations.

It pays to be as precise as possible when identifying needs.

RECOGNISING TRAINING NEEDS

AVOID GENERALISATION

$\boxed{M}$ As a **manager** you can help by being as specific as possible in describing the need. This will eventually save you time and money because needs can often be met in ways other than sending people on courses. (See pages 45-54 for techniques.)

$\boxed{T}$ Should you be a **trainer,** trying to respond to needs, probe behind any general statements for a more accurate description. Only then can you do something useful.

Tip: look at job descriptions for details of knowledge and skills that individuals need. Alternatively, initiatives — in the UK — such as Management Charter and (S)NVQ can be used as the basis for identifying abilities and spotting needs.

RECOGNISING TRAINING NEEDS

LEARNING GAP

Accurate identification of **needs** will reveal a **learning gap** between present knowledge and skill, and the desired level.

PRESENT KNOWLEDGE AND SKILLS)) LEARNING GAP ((DESIRED LEVEL OF KNOWLEDGE AND SKILLS

As an aid to motivation — as well as getting people to own their development — spend time both identifying and agreeing the gap with those involved, ie:

- why do they think that it has occurred?
- how do they think that the gap can be closed?
- what support do they want?

NEEDS INTO OBJECTIVES

REASONS FOR OBJECTIVES

Having identified a need try turning it into a learning objective. In other words what **noticeable behaviour** will you see when the learning has taken place?

Why? As a basis for:

- ensuring that the training reflects the needs of the organisation

- measuring the outcome of any learning (otherwise how will you know that you have achieved the desired result?)

- motivating the learner to **know** what they have to achieve

- demonstrating the payoff to organisation and individual

- any cost benefit analysis that you do

- starting the design of any learning event.

NEEDS INTO OBJECTIVES

WRITING LEARNING OBJECTIVES

Objectives are needed to show what, at the end of the learning, individuals will:

- **Know,** eg: how to organise a particular event.

- **Be able to do** (that requires the acquisition or development of **skills**),
  eg: be able to persuade, assemble, draw, etc.

- To each of these needs to be added some form of **measurement** of the
  effective behaviour.

There may also be times when you have to describe the conditions under which
people are expected to operate.

Note: beware of objectives that claim to improve or change attitudes.
Attitudes often show themselves in people's behaviour; it is the behaviour that
you need to concentrate on changing or adapting.

NEEDS INTO OBJECTIVES

WRITING LEARNING OBJECTIVES

Take the **need** that you have identified and ask:

— what has to be done?

— to what standard, and

— by when?

Concentrate on what the **end result** of the actions will be and use verbs and/or action words such as:

— **describe, identify, organise**

— **assemble, persuade, show.**

It's acceptable to have more than one verb or action word in an objective.

NEEDS INTO OBJECTIVES

EXAMPLE: TIME MANAGEMENT

1 Identify the Need

Your people need to improve their use and management of time. This has shown itself by individuals:

- working long hours

- getting side-tracked by interruptions

- taking on too many jobs

- failing to meet deadlines.

NEEDS INTO OBJECTIVES

EXAMPLE: TIME MANAGEMENT

2 Establish the Evidence

If you are designing some training in this area, ask yourself:
— what will I accept as evidence that I have succeeded?
(What you come up with **is** the objective.)

The evidence could be that individuals will:

Know
- the basic principles of managing their time
- how to organise both themselves and others
- how to select objectives/priorities on which to work.

Be able to
- prioritise their work
- organise themselves to achieve priorities
- use a time log to identify how their time is spent
- deal effectively with interruptions.

NEEDS INTO OBJECTIVES

EXAMPLE: TIME MANAGEMENT

3 Write the Objectives

Objectives for a course you put together might look as follows.

At the end of the course individuals will be able to:

- establish the content of their job and will have identified 3 priority objectives to achieve over the next 3 months

- devise plans for achieving these objectives with key dates identified in their diary

- operate a system for examining their use of time and state ways in which they can take control over their daily activities.

NEEDS INTO OBJECTIVES

EXAMPLE: PROBLEM SOLVING/CREATIVITY

1 Identify the need

You need to help people improve their skills in dealing with problems and thinking afresh.

This has become evident through:

- lack of new ideas coming forward within the organisation

- groups spending a lot of time dealing with the symptoms of problems and failing to get to the root cause (drowning in problems)

- the organisation's need for new products/services in order to keep ahead of the market

- a change management programme going through.

NEEDS INTO OBJECTIVES

EXAMPLE: PROBLEM SOLVING/CREATIVITY

2 Establish the Evidence

Evidence of success might be that individuals:

Know	• how to apply a structured approach to solving problems
	• how to distinguish between the symptoms of a problem and its cause
	• a range of creativity techniques to help them generate ideas.
Are able to	• operate a structured approach to solving a problem they are facing
	• generate new ideas for tackling situations
	• sell their ideas to others.

NEEDS INTO OBJECTIVES

EXAMPLE: PROBLEM SOLVING/CREATIVITY

3 Write the Objectives

Objectives for a course might be that, at the end, individuals will:

- be able to recognise the benefits that being creative can bring (to both the organisation and the job)

- have identified 3 areas where fresh thinking can be applied to their job

- be able to apply a structured approach to a current business problem/opportunity and have generated a minimum of 3 new ways of tackling it

- plan how they are going to sell their ideas to others upon their return to work.

NEEDS INTO OBJECTIVES

OBJECTIVES NOT AIMS

$\boxed{T}$ Tips for trainers— beware of vague objectives.

When buying in training carefully study the objectives of any proposal to see if they are expressed in terms of behavioural outcomes. If not, then ask the provider to explain how you will know that their training has been successful.

Very often what are stated as objectives are really aims.
Aims are directions, objectives are destinations.

NEEDS INTO OBJECTIVES

CHECKLIST

- Identify training required

- Ask yourself what you want people to be able to do as a result of the training

- Establish evidence of success

- Try writing some draft objectives
  — check them against the need and evidence of success
  — should they not quite fit then have another go

FINDING LEARNING OPPORTUNITIES

LEARNING IS ALL AROUND US

- Both 'life' and 'work' offer endless opportunities to learn.
  All too often, organisations restrict themselves to course or classroom
  learning activities (despite the ineffectiveness of the process and the
  comments of those attending)

- Look for opportunities both on and off the job (see next page)

- What you end up selecting depends on a variety of factors:
  - the precise nature of the need
  - timescale . . . . . how urgent is it?
  - availability of people to give and receive any planned help
  - costs involved, facilities required
  - preferred style of the learner (see pages 85-88 on learning style)

FINDING LEARNING OPPORTUNITIES

WITHIN WORK

Learning opportunities at work include:

Within job
- attending meetings
- projects
- making a presentation
- acting as a spokesperson
- writing a report
- visiting a supplier
- showing people around

Extending the job
- standing in for somebody
- shadowing/work experience
- job sharing
- some form of exchange
- secondment
- job rotation

FINDING LEARNING OPPORTUNITIES

WITHIN WORK

Extra responsibility
- taking on added responsibilities
- setting something up
- closing something down
- being promoted

Working with others
- passing on skills/experience to others
- being part of a project team, task force, quality circle
- introducing a change
- putting together a training programme
- being involved in negotiations

As well as. . . .
- watching somebody in action (an expert or skilled performer)
- spending time with an expert
- being thrown in at the deep end
- crises
- from successes and disasters

TRAINING TECHNIQUES

The following pages set out nine different methods of training, with some of their attendant advantages and disadvantages.

1 Coaching

A process in which a manager, through direct discussion, helps a colleague to learn to solve a problem or do a task. It can work in conjunction with counselling for performance improvement.

Pros	Cons
Can be any two managers/individuals, not simply boss and subordinate	Style used by 'boss', eg: directive may affect its outcome
Problem orientated approach; thus involves a problem solving process	Carried out effectively, it requires a considerable level of skill from both parties
Quick to set up	
Builds on actual situation	Results may take some time to achieve
Can develop both individuals	

TRAINING TECHNIQUES

2 Action Learning

Where groups of individuals come together to work on real life organisational problems.

Pros	Cons

Pros

Involves those best qualified to solve problems and those who have them

Best opportunity to develop individuals is in their own organisation

Is action based and immediate, not concerned with making future recommendations

Cons

To work well it needs a certain amount of structure

Relies on people being open and prepared to share their situations with others

Possibly suffers from an image problem — in that it is still not as widely used as it could be

46

FINDING LEARNING OPPORTUNITIES

TRAINING TECHNIQUES

3 Role Play

A technique used to rehearse the skills needed in certain situations.

Pros	Cons
Individual takes on some of the feelings and attitudes associated with the role	Relies on a person being able to play a 'role' effectively
Enables people to play out solutions and experience the other point of view	Individual may need to be coached through role plays to get the most out of them
Can be used for a variety of situations, ie: practising a skill, demonstrating a situation or trying out intended actions	For some people it can be an alarming experience

TRAINING TECHNIQUES

4 Internal courses

Where individuals from the same organisation come together to develop their
skills and abilities.

Pros	**Cons**
Trains a large number of people at one time	Chance for individuals to complain about the organisation (group moan)
Content can be made directly relevant to organisation	No exposure to 'fresh thinking' from fellow participants outside their organisation
Can help shape opinions and work towards changing attitudes	Without help and support from managers, there's no guarantee that knowledge and skills will be applied
Aids promotion of a common message	

FINDING LEARNING OPPORTUNITIES

TRAINING TECHNIQUES

5 External courses

Attended by people from a variety of organisations.

Pros

Exposure to fresh thinking

Chance to meet
new people and
share ideas

Can make people
appreciate what a
good organisation
they work for

Cons

Expensive

Content may be too general to be of
any relevance

Again, no guarantee that ideas
gained can be applied without
support in the organisation

TRAINING TECHNIQUES

6 Delegating tasks

Whereby a manager gives up part of their job to another person.

Pros	Cons
Shows trust and confidence in individuals	Is hard work and requires confidence and faith in others
Frees the manager to do more valuable work	Involves committing time in the short term for a longer term payoff
Useful way of developing — with guidance — the skills of staff	Staff capable of taking delegation may be in short supply

Note: Delegation and empowerment are not the same. Empowerment involves removing constraints which prevent someone from doing their job as effectively as possible.

TRAINING TECHNIQUES

7 Video

On a particular topic relevant to the organisation or a job.

Pros	**Cons**
Can be entertaining and informative	Expensive to produce, buy or hire
Multi-use for a large number of people	Not everybody may find them of interest
Can be shown at any time of the day/night as well as in work/non work locations	No guarantee that individuals will be able to identify with the situation or apply the messages

TRAINING TECHNIQUES

8 One-to-one

Where individuals receive direct instruction from another. This could be working with or watching an acknowledged expert, or simply 'sitting next to Nelly'.

Pros	Cons
Allows individuals to learn from a competent performer	'Expert' may be a poor tutor
Often quick, easy and cheap to set up	Relies upon the learner to take the initiative and ask for explanation
Has the potential to impart a great deal of knowledge in a short period of time	Can be unstructured . . . "go and watch and see how they do it". If so, learning is often by chance and not design

TRAINING TECHNIQUES

9 Open or Flexible Learning

A generic term used to refer to a wide range of approaches, where the learner has a choice over what and how they learn, as well as the pace and the time.

It is a fast developing area that embraces a range of learning approaches, including:

- workbooks (often supported by audio and video material)

- technology based training, such as computer assisted learning, interactive video and CD Rom. (Many software packages include on-screen tutorials.)

Off-the-shelf programmes are available from an increasing number of suppliers. Alternatively, it is possible to have materials produced to suit your own needs.

TRAINING TECHNIQUES

9 Open or Flexible Learning (cont'd)

Costs of setting up the location, equipment and materials can often be high.

Furthermore, open or flexible learning is not tutor free. Help is needed to explain, support, guide and encourage the learner. This calls for different skills from that of the 'up front' classroom presenter.

However, the many advantages of this approach include:

- being able to train staff in various locations
- targeting and equipping (often vast numbers of staff) with the specific skills needed to keep ahead in business
- the potential to be significantly cheaper than conventional (course based) training.

For a comprehensive guide to learning methods see the 'Encyclopaedia of Management Development Methods' by Andrzej Huczynski published by Gower.

TRANSFER OF LEARNING

A note of caution!

- Whatever the method you use do not assume that people will **automatically** be able to use their new found knowledge and skills in their own situation. Sadly, it is not always that easy. So ....

- When selecting methods think also about how you plan to ensure the transfer of any learning gained, and **build it into your design stage.**

- Guidelines include as far as practicable:
  — trying to keep training situations and job similar
  — always making a link between training and the job that they are/will be doing
  — showing what will be the reward — in the workplace — for using the knowledge and skills
  — aiding retention by helping people to try out the skills learnt **sooner rather than later.**

TRANSFER OF LEARNING POTENTIAL

Assuming that the methods chosen are appropriate to the individuals' needs, transfer of learning potential can be increased in each of the areas by:

Coaching	see person in action; give further ideas and encouragement if needed
Action Learning	give individuals chance to try out new approaches and ideas
Role play	make situations as real as possible
Courses (internal and external)	be clear in advance about content; ensure that pre and post course briefings take place, and coach people to use what they have learnt
Delegation	invest time in the learning stage plus watch them in action
Video	carefully select the video; link any message in it to the needs of organisation/individual
One-to-one	make sure learner is aware of why and how things happen; if relevant give them a chance to practise with guidance
Open Learning	look for opportunities where learner can use their knowledge and skills with support.

PREPARING FOR LEARNING

BRIEFING THE LEARNER
HOW NOT TO

1   Manager passes on details of a training event without:
    — understanding what it's about
    — checking the relevance to trainee and job
    — talking to the individual.

2   Individual attends:
    — not knowing what it's about
    — anti or indifferent to the learning (a trainer's nightmare)
    — sees no relevance in the topics or their applications
    — disrupts the event with negative comments,
      eg: 'you should tell all this to my boss, not me'
    — feels slightly inferior to others who are clearly
      there for a purpose.

3   Resulting in a:
    — negative experience all round
    — waste of time and money
    — missed opportunity for all.

BRIEFING THE LEARNER
THE MANAGER'S ROLE

$\boxed{M}$ If you are a manager you need to be involved in briefing people.

- You may have helped identify the need and suggested a solution.
- As part of your day-to-day role as coach, you need to ensure that your staff have the opportunity to **use** any knowledge and skills gained, when they return to work.
- Without the chance to practise and apply (under your guidance) any new found learning, it will all have been a wasted effort.
- You may learn something yourself.

$\boxed{T}$ If you are a trainer you need to get the managers involved:

- because they are part of the learning process (see above)
- because they can ensure the transfer of learning.

BRIEFING THE LEARNER
WHAT TO TELL THEM

$\boxed{M}$ It is **essential** that individuals are briefed — preferably by their manager — before any learning activities take place. Explain:

- what has been arranged for them, and in what form
- the reasons why — link to possible changes taking place, appraisals, requests for help or career development
- how it is designed to help them, the links between the learning and practical application
- what it will involve (content, style of learning, action plans)
- where it will take place (venue, timing, dates, expenses and — if relevant — travel arrangements and accommodation)
- any reporting back that may take place
- what help they will get, on return, to apply the learning.

Note: If you are unable to answer any of these questions then go back and ask the provider of the training. Remember training is not cheap.

PREPARING FOR LEARNING

BRIEFING THE LEARNER
BEFORE A COURSE

$\boxed{M}$ I have seen the following training nomination form used to good effect in an organisation for those attending formal training courses.

The aim is to ensure that managers become involved before the event by

ensuring that they have briefed their staff.

$\boxed{T}$ If you are a trainer you may care to use it as the basis for designing your own.

PREPARING FOR LEARNING

TRAINING NOMINATION FORM

Instructions

1   Form to be completed by the nominated manager.
2   Discussed with the member of staff and their responses noted.
3   Returned to the training department before the event.

Name   ....
Position   .... Department ....
Course title .... Date(s) ....

1   Reasons for nominating the above for the course are to:
     a) Improve the skills needed for their present job   Yes/No
     b) Provide a broader understanding and knowledge
        of the subject area   Yes/No
     c) Personal development   Yes/No

Any other reasons

....
....

PREPARING FOR LEARNING

TRAINING NOMINATION FORM

2   Has the member of staff been informed of:
    a) The course title and objectives?   Yes/No
    b) Why they have been selected to attend?   Yes/No

3   Is the member of staff:
    a) Enthusiastic about attending?   Yes/No
    b) Indifferent about attending? **   Yes/No
    c) Reluctant about attending?   Yes/No
    d) Other (please comment)
** if the answer to b) or c) is 'yes' could you expand on the reasons

. . . .
. . . .

4   Has the individual had any previous instruction or training in the subject
    matter covered by the course?   Yes/No
    If the answer is 'yes' then please give an indication of the level and
    extent so that the training can be matched to experience . . . .
. . . .

PREPARING FOR LEARNING

TRAINING NOMINATION FORM

5   What do you expect the learning to do for your member of staff and <u>why</u>?

. . . .

6   How do you plan to ensure that these expectations are met?

. . . .

7   What plans have you agreed with the member of staff to enable them to use
    the skills and/or knowledge they have learnt back in the workplace?

. . . .

<u>Please return completed form to (nominated person) by (date).</u>

BRIEFING THE TRAINER

Useful information that a trainer (internal or external) needs to know before starting includes:

- the big picture, ie: what's happening in the organisation and any current or potential issues that might be raised in the training (it may help them to make links between the training and the bigger picture)

- who's attending?
  — what jobs they do and where
  — any relevant information about their background, skills and previous experiences; whether or not they all know one another
  — why they have been nominated to attend and what they want out of it
  — any concerns that may have been expressed to you beforehand.

PREPARING FOR LEARNING

RUNNING A COURSE

$\boxed{M}$ If you are a manager who has organised a course or event for your staff, then:

- It's worth being around at the start to:
  — ensure that the rooms are set up as requested; handouts, notes are available
  — welcome people and show them where things are
  — make sure that any planned refreshments have arrived
  — make contact with the speakers
  — formally introduce the speaker, explain any in-house routines, including the taking of messages.

PREPARING FOR LEARNING

RUNNING A COURSE

- You should check during the day, to:
  - see how the speaker is performing
  - is he/she doing what was agreed?
  - how are people reacting to the speaker and to each other?
  - what's the mood? (Try joining them for lunch although don't expect much useful information on the learning to come out).

- Then attend at the end, to:
  - wrap it up and explain what will happen next
  - gain the views of the participants (again don't expect too much as it may be too soon; very often participants do their thinking on the journey home)
  - talk things through with the speaker
  - be aware of any contentious views that have emerged from or during the day.

PREPARING FOR LEARNING

LET'S RECAP

To get a return on your investment do what you can to make people aware of:

- what has been arranged for them and why
- how it will help them
- how they will be helped to apply the learning.

Don't rely on luck. Both managers and trainers have a key role to play in preparing their people for learning.

WHO TO USE

WHO TO USE

INTERNAL

Firstly look to yourself, and the resources within your organisation.

Pros

- know the organisation, its culture and often the people

- cost — they are already on the payroll

- saves time — needs can often be met sooner rather than later

- by sharing their knowledge and expertise they also develop their own skills

Cons

- can be too familiar with people

- too busy — may have insufficient time to prepare

- may not be trained as 'teachers' — could be technically sound but poor at putting it across

- not necessarily good role models — do as I say not as I do

WHO TO USE

INTERNAL
SEE THEM IN ACTION

Remember . . . . . .

- People can be trained to 'teach'.
  (The Management Pocketbook series has many titles to help. See
  particularly *The Instructor's Pocketbook* and *Challengers!* for training
  delivery, and *The Trainer's Pocketbook* and *The Team Builder's Pocketfile*
  for exercises to use in your own events. Details on pp 108-9.)

- If you do use internal resources then:
  — try to see them in action (how good are they at 'helping'?)
  — make sure they know the skills your people **need** to learn

- Jointly explore the best ways of making this happen.

WHO TO USE

EXTERNAL
10 QUESTIONS TO ASK

Bringing people in from outside can be both expensive and risky. It's an area where it is easy to make mistakes, waste an awful lot of money and get it badly wrong.

However, if you get it right then there are many benefits to be gained on both sides. As with identifying needs, it pays to devote time to selecting the right providers.

Questions to ask:
1   What are they offering (standard courses, tailor-made, computer assisted learning, etc.)?

2   What is their knowledge and understanding of your business and the market in which you operate? (This is not a pre-requisite but often a useful indicator to see how much they have bothered to find out about your organisation.)

EXTERNAL
10 QUESTIONS TO ASK

3 About any proposal that they make:
  - does it make sense?
  - what does it cover, and how far does it reflect your needs and/or any brief that you have given them?

4 Who will be involved in delivering any training?
  - what are their credentials and experience?

  - what back up is there, should there be a problem?

5 If you are not talking to the training deliverer, when will you meet him or her? (73)

EXTERNAL
10 QUESTIONS TO ASK

6   Of the organisation (and indeed the individual):
- what are they known for?
- what have they researched, written and had published?

7   Learning methods
- how do they teach? (suitable for all styles?)
- what materials do they use and what's the basis for it? (some of the motivation theories are pretty old and the research data rather suspect)

8   Who else have they done similar work for?
- what **exactly** did they do, when, where?
- who can you contact in that organisation so that you can hear **their** version of how it went?

WHO TO USE

EXTERNAL
10 QUESTIONS TO ASK

9 What will it cost?
   - for any fees quoted what **exactly** do they cover?
   - hidden costs could include
     — development work
     — putting together the proposal
     — visits and attending meetings
     — travel (at what rate .... yours or theirs?)
     — accommodation (what will you pay for?)
     — 'expenses': what does this include/not include?
     — has the meter already started?
   - don't forget to add on any tax
   - does it sound good value for money?
   - how far will it stack up against any cost/benefit analysis?

EXTERNAL
10 QUESTIONS TO ASK

10   What are they going to do to find out about your organisation **at their expense?**

- Finally, a question for you. What's your 'gut reaction' about them and their organisation? Are they credible? Could you and your people work with them . . . . how will they be accepted?

BEWARE OF EXPERTS

There are plenty of so called 'experts' offering help. Be on your guard against:

- the glossy brochure with stage managed photos
  — 'perfect' people in smart clothes
  — meaningless graphs on the flip charts
  — everybody paying attention to the charismatic tutor (not even **I** can hold attention like their presenters claim to!!)

- the impressive client list
  — what **exactly** did they do, and for what parts of this (impressive) organisation
  — the promises and claims to do everything
  — the training flavour of the month
  — the salesperson who sells the concept or idea, that's delivered by someone else you have never met.

WHERE TO FIND HELP

- They may well come to you via:
  — mailshots
  — speculative calls by phone or in person
  — contacts
  — recommendations
  — personal experience (you have seen them in action).

- You can get names from:
  — professional organisations, ie: Institute of Management Consultants and The Institute of Personnel and Development
  — your own contacts in other organisations
  — articles (or books) that they have written, publicising their success and skills
  — training directories in libraries; visits to trade fairs and exhibitions.

WHO TO USE

WHAT TO LOOK FOR IN A TRAINER

As a guide, look for individuals who can demonstrate:

1 Competence in and knowledge of the subject
2 The ability to put it across in a variety of situations
3 Concern/empathy for students' learning problems.

The professional trainer demonstrates a high level of skills
in each of these areas, in particular finding time to:

— empathise
— adapt his or her material to groups or individuals
— coach and counsel, even if it involves working through breaks and after
  sessions.

(Source John Townsend Journal of European Industrial Training Vol 3 No 1985)

MAINTAINING A FRESH APPROACH

$\boxed{T}$ Do you use the same people every year to provide training for you?
This way your trainers get to know your organisation and its needs.
The danger, though, is that they might become complacent, stale and take you for granted. So, try putting your training out for tender say every couple of years.
Invite a range of people to suggest ways in which they would tackle your needs.
This allows you to:

- test the market and get fresh ideas

- ask some of the questions suggested on pages 72 to 76

- ensure that you are getting what your organisation needs

- involve others (especially line managers) in the selection process

- keep your existing providers on their toes!

INCREASING YOUR CHANCES

INFLUENCING THE CONTENT

You can increase your chances of getting results from your training if you can get the trainer to deliver what your people need, as opposed to what he/she **likes** to deliver.

If training needs and objectives are based around the trainer's choices, sessions are likely to be:

- formal and taught
- well planned, yet kept strictly to a timetable
- led from the front, with little involvement from the learner.

By asking individuals what they want, and accommodating their requests, the **learner** becomes the centre of attention and as a result can become:

- more actively involved
- in control of what they learn, and
- motivated to develop themselves.

LEARNER CENTRED TRAINING

Learner centred training calls for:
- a different relationship between 'trainer' (whether line manager or professional trainer) and trainee, ie: 'how can I help you?' as opposed to 'listen to this . . . . .')

- less emphasis on the trainer's 'instructional' skills; more focus on a supportive, guiding, coaching role.

$\boxed{T}$ Trainers: your organisation may well be going down the route of self development. This puts the focus on the individual and asks what they need to do to improve themselves.

As a result, you could find yourself running/organising fewer formal courses and encouraging more 'open learning initiatives' and on-the-job opportunities.

INCREASING YOUR CHANCES

HELPING PEOPLE LEARN

First of all it is important to recognise:

- the differences between you and the learner(s) in terms of:
  — age
  — experience
  — position/status
  — skills, knowledge and experience
  — contacts in the organisation

- the uniqueness of the situation
  — one off?

- people's preferred learning styles
  — what works for you may not work for them and vice versa.

TRAINING FAILURES
WHAT WENT WRONG?

The following four case studies describe people who gained little from the training organised for them.

Person A:
a lively outgoing individual always keen to try new experiences, was sent on a course that involved listening to lectures, reading the accompanying notes in a manual, and watching videos.

Person B:
a quieter, more cautious, individual, has a preference for sitting back and watching others, preferring to think before acting. As part of his development he was sent on an outdoor leadership event. The course involved being selected at short notice to lead a team. Feedback on his performance was then given by both instructors and fellow team members.

TRAINING FAILURES
WHAT WENT WRONG?

Person C:
could be described as a perfectionist, with a tendency to think things through in a logical step-by-step way, whilst questioning and probing the basic assumptions behind something.

As part of improving her relationships with others, she was asked to attend a sensitivity training programme. An integral part of this involved opening up to situations she was facing and talking through her feelings.

Person D:
is practical and is always looking for new techniques or ideas to try out in the job. He was sent on training where individuals were not encouraged to make links between the content and their own jobs. Consequently he described it as too 'ivory tower' and of little practical use.

LEARNING STYLES
PREFERENCES REVEALED

Training often fails— the causes are varied, and many cannot be controlled. However, one potential problem area is if the method of learning to which individuals are exposed does not suit their preferred style. Honey and Mumford's work on learning styles identified:

- **activists** (Person A) who:
  — learn best from short here-and-now tasks
  — try anything once and are enthusiastic about new activities
  — throw themselves into action based courses, games and exercises, especially anything competitive.

- **reflectors** (Person B) who:
  — learn best from standing back and observing what's happening
  — prefer to collect and analyse data before coming to conclusions
  — enjoy watching people in action.

LEARNING STYLES
PREFERENCES REVEALED

- **theorists** (Person C) who:
    - learn best when reviewing content in terms of a system, model or theory
    - tend to be detached and analytical
    - put great stock on rationality and logic.

- **pragmatists** (Person D) who:
    - learn when there is an obvious link between the subject matter and a problem or opportunity on the job
    - search for new ideas and the chance to apply them to a relevant situation
    - like to get on with things, rather than have long open-ended discussions.

INCREASING YOUR CHANCES

IMPLICATIONS FOR LEARNING

$\boxed{M}$ If you are a manager or supervisor looking to organise training for others:

- Bear in mind your own preferences
  — **don't let this influence how you organise learning for others**.
    Remember, we are all different.

- Ask individuals for their own experiences
  — this could give you a clue to their preferred style and, more importantly,
    influence the type of learning experiences you put together.

$\boxed{T}$ Trainers: try putting people through the Honey and Mumford Learning Styles
Questionnaire before arranging any training. *(See the reading list for details.)*

It could well shape what you do for people and the composition of the learning
groups. **More importantly it could significantly increase your chances of success
and impact.**

HELPING OLDER LEARNERS

If you are organising training for older workers they may need something different. Should this be the case, then try to:

- keep memorising to a minimum

- use understanding as the basis for learning wherever possible

- with physical skills, concentrate on speed and accuracy, using simple tests

- give practical experience before theory— if at all possible

- where precise physical movements are needed, use 'hands over', ie: guide the hand

- ensure a high success rate in the early stages of learning

- arrange for an older learner to have an experienced worker as nominated 'friend'.

DON'T FORGET

We have learnt to do many things in our lives, eg: in the home or by following some form of hobby or interest. **Hardly any of it takes place in a formal classroom environment.**

INCREASING YOUR CHANCES

THE NEXT STEP

So, having taken action to increase your chances of success, you should now be in a position to run effective learning events.

However, this is **not** the end of the story.

You still have to work out how you are going to measure the impact on performance of what you have set up.

MEASURING THE IMPACT

WHAT HAPPENS IN PRACTICE

A lot of effort, time and money goes into planning and running a training event. However, attempts at evaluating the impact that it has had on performance are often given little consideration.

Examples in this area include:

— doing nothing at all
— a 'tick in the box' form; the categories of which are often so generalised as to be meaningless
— a form that focuses more on the admin details than what people have learnt
— a form which delegates are asked to complete at the end of the training. The danger with this approach is that people are often in a hurry to leave, and have simply 'had enough'.

Evaluation criteria, as well as methods, need to be established and included in the setting of objectives/learning design phase.

MEASURING THE IMPACT

ASSESSMENT OR EVALUATION?

There are two fundamental elements of training:

1. The quality of the training that takes place.
   Eg: how much people enjoyed it, what exercises were used and the standard of the venue.
   The quality of these aspects can be **assessed** by such things as questionnaires and talking to people.

2. The quality and value of what people have learnt as a result.
   Eg: what learning has taken place, how people have changed, and the personal benefits in terms of behaviour and performance.
   The value or worth of these can be **evaluated**.

For more information in this area read *'The Business of Training'* by Trevor Bentley published by McGraw-Hill.

MEASURING THE IMPACT

THE CASE FOR EVALUATION

$\boxed{T}$ Evaluation of what has been learnt is extremely important. If you are a trainer in an organisation it helps you to demonstrate:

- the number of training days provided

- the costs and benefits to the organisation

- the contribution that training has made in terms of
  — the achievement of specific business or organisational goals
  — improvements in productivity and performance
  — impact on 'bottom line' where feasible
  — how satisfied your customers are, especially if training is seen as a service department.

Don't forget to evaluate all forms of training, not just courses.

MEASURING THE IMPACT

THE CASE FOR EVALUATION

$\boxed{T}$ You may also need objective evidence:

- to compose a budget
- to justify expenditure and secure additional resources
- to identify what percentage of salary costs are spent on training
- to make comparisons with other organisations
- as a basis for publicising your work, either internally or externally, via a company report.

$\boxed{M}$ As a manager you will want to know the return on your investment. You will always get comments about the venue, food, tutor. Far **more** value will be obtained from the quality of the learning that has resulted:

— what can they do now that they could not do before?
— what measurable changes in performance has it produced?
— overall was the effort worthwhile?

TECHNIQUES FOR EVALUATION

The value and worth of training can be measured both whilst learning is taking place and afterwards.

1   Within learning events

Aim: to find out what people are learning.

For example, use questionnaires to identify:

- what people know at the start of a learning event
- to check their understanding of learning points during an event
- to test what they have acquired at the end.

A whole range of quizzes can be devised to recap any points made during the learning. These are often a lot of fun for participants, as well as serving to provide a valuable reinforcement of the learning.

For more details see 'The Trainer's Pocketbook of ready-to-use exercises' by John Townsend published by Management Pocketbooks Ltd.

TECHNIQUES FOR EVALUATION

2 End of learning

Aim: to assess the trainee's opinion of the training received.

This is often carried out by the training department in the form of a questionnaire (see example on page 103).

However, managers have a key role to play at this stage by **talking** to their people in order to:

- start to evaluate the worth of the training, and importantly ....

- create a receptive environment, to encourage individuals to use their newly acquired knowledge and skills in the workplace.

TECHNIQUES FOR EVALUATION

3   What has been learnt

Aim: to measure the concepts, skills and techniques that the individual has acquired.

Again, this need not be the job of the training manager. The person who has run the 'learning event' can help in devising methods to assess this area. What better way to judge how effective their teaching has been?

 The **manager** can help by setting up job simulations or role plays in order to practise skills. For example, if the learning has focused on dealing with difficult customers, why not set up some simple scenarios to develop further the skills gained.

TECHNIQUES FOR EVALUATION

4   Measuring resulting improvements

Aim: to discover how the individual has improved in their job as a result of the training they have received.

One way to do this is a three month follow up, involving the trainer, the manager and the trainee.

Useful techniques involve making comparisons before and after the learning, as well as observing changes in behaviour.

TECHNIQUES FOR EVALUATION

5   Impact on the organisation

Aim: to identify the benefits gained in terms of money, time and resources invested.

$\boxed{T}$ Often carried out by the trainer, it seeks to demonstrate the value of the training to the organisation.

Areas to look at include:

- improvements in work output
- cost savings
- error rates
- reduction in the number and nature of complaints
- improvements in quality
- staff attitude changes.

MEASURING THE IMPACT

COURSE EVALUATION FORM
EXAMPLE

Course Title . . . .
Dates . . . .

Name . . . . Place of work . . . . Phone No . . . .

We would appreciate feedback on the recent course that you attended. This will
enable us to assess its usefulness and value to the organisation. Please be
honest with your comments.

1 In what way was the course relevant to you? . . . .

2 What areas were not relevant to you? . . . .

3 Which subjects/sessions did you personally find **most** useful? . . . .

  Why? . . . .

4 Which subject/sessions did you find **least** useful? . . . .

  Why? . . . .

(103)

MEASURING THE IMPACT

COURSE EVALUATION FORM
EXAMPLE

5 How do you plan to put any useful learning gained into practice? . . . .

. . . .

6 To apply the learning, what help do you require from?
Your boss   . . . .
Your colleagues or staff   . . . .
Training staff   . . . .
From others (please specify)   . . . .

7 What other comments do you wish to make about the training?

. . . .

8 Overall do you feel that the course was worthwhile, in terms of your time away from work? Yes . . . . No . . . . . . Unsure . . . .

(104) Thank you for your comments, please return this form to: . . . .

WHAT STOPS PEOPLE LEARNING?

Finally, if you feel that you have done everything right and people still do not seem to be learning — then there could be **learning blockages,** or hurdles, outside of your control.
For example:

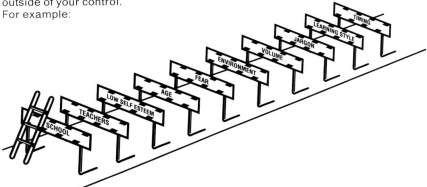

FURTHER READING

'The Business of Training' by Trevor Bentley *published by McGraw-Hill*

'Evaluating Training Effectiveness' by Peter Bramley *published by McGraw-Hill*

'Improving Trainer Effectiveness' edited by Roger Bennett *published by Gower*

'The Theory and Practice of Training' by Roger Buckley and Jim Caple
published by Kogan Page

'Evaluation: Relating Training to Business Performance' by Terence Jackson
published by Kogan Page

'Management Development— Strategies for Action' by Alan Mumford
published by The Institute of Personnel Management

'The Manual of Learning Styles' by Peter Honey and Alan Mumford
obtainable from Ardingly House, 10 Linden Avenue, Maidenhead, Berks

A whole range of books by John Townsend published under the Management
Pocketbook series that are suitable for both the ad hoc and professional trainer.
 See following pages for details.

Other titles in the Pocketbook series include:

The Manager's Pocketbook, **The Teamworking Pocketbook** (illustrated),
The People Manager's Pocketbook and **The Appraisals Pocketbook**.

THE MANAGEMENT POCKETBOOK SERIES

Pocketbooks

Appraisals Pocketbook
Assertiveness Pocketbook
Balance Sheet Pocketbook
Business Planning Pocketbook
Business Presenter's Pocketbook
Business Writing Pocketbook
Challengers Pocketbook
Coaching Pocketbook
Communicator's Pocketbook
Creative Manager's Pocketbook
Cross-cultural Business Pocketbook
Cultural Gaffes Pocketbook
Customer Service Pocketbook
Empowerment Pocketbook
Export Pocketbook
Facilitator's Pocketbook
Improving Profitability Pocketbook
Interviewer's Pocketbook
Key Account Manager's Pocketbook
Learner's Pocketbook

Managing Budgets Pocketbook
Managing Cashflow Pocketbook
Managing Change Pocketbook
Managing Your Appraisal Pocketbook
Manager's Pocketbook
Manager's Training Pocketbook
Marketing Pocketbook
Meetings Pocketbook
Mentoring Pocketbook
Motivation Pocketbook
Negotiator's Pocketbook
People Manager's Pocketbook
Performance Management Pocketbook
Personal Success Pocketbook
Problem Behaviour Pocketbook
Project Management Pocketbook
Quality Pocketbook
Sales Excellence Pocketbook
Salesperson's Pocketbook
Self-managed Development Pocketbook
Stress Pocketbook

Teamworking Pocketbook
Telephone Skills Pocketbook
Telesales Pocketbook
Thinker's Pocketbook
Time Management Pocketbook
Trainer Standards Pocketbook
Trainer's Pocketbook

Pocketfiles/Other

Leadership: Sharing The Passion
The Great Presentation Scandal
Trainer's Blue Pocketfile of
Ready-to-use Exercises
Trainer's Green Pocketfile of
Ready-to-use Exercises
Trainer's Red Pocketfile of
Ready-to-use Exercises

Audio Cassettes

Tips for Presenters
Tips for Trainers

About the Author

Ian Fleming, MA, DMS, DipEd

Ian is a freelance management trainer. His approach is to work mainly in-company, helping managers and their teams tackle real situations and opportunities. He has a preference for coaching rather than lecturing.

This pocketbook is the result of working with managers tackling similar situations. It complements his other titles in the pocketbook series on time management, teamworking, coaching and manager's training.

Contact

Should you want to talk to Ian about his ideas and approach, he can be contacted at: 2 Robins Orchard, Chalfont St Peter, Buckinghamshire, SL9 0HQ
Tel: 01494 873623   Fax: 01494 875959   E-mail: ian@creativelearning.demon.co.uk

Published by: Management Pocketbooks Ltd 14 East Street, Alresford, Hants SO24 9EE, U.K.
Tel: +44 (0)1962 735573   Fax: +44 (0)1962 733637   E-mail: pocketbks@aol.com
Web: www.pocketbook.co.uk

All rights reserved

© Copyright Ian Fleming 1994. First published in 1994. Reprinted 1997, 1999.

British Library Cataloguing-in-Publication Data – A catalogue record for this book is available from the British Library.

Printed in U.K. by: Alresford Press Ltd, Prospect Road, Alresford, Hants   ISBN 1 870471 23 7

ORDER FORM

Your details

Name _____

Position _____

Company _____

Address _____

_____

Telephone _____

Facsimile _____

E-mail _____

VAT No. (EC companies) _____

Your Order Ref _____

Please send me:

		No. copies
The Manager's Training	Pocketbook	
The _____	Pocketbook	
The _____	Pocketbook	
The _____	Pocketbook	
The _____	Pocketbook	

Order by Post

MANAGEMENT POCKETBOOKS LTD
14 EAST STREET ALRESFORD HAMPSHIRE SO24 9EE UK

Order by Phone, Fax or Internet

Telephone: +44 (0)1962 735573
Facsimile: +44 (0)1962 733637
E-mail: pocketbks@aol.com
Web: www.pocketbook.co.uk

Customers in USA should contact:
Stylus Publishing, LLC
22883 Quicksilver Drive, Sterling, VA 20166-2012
Telephone: 703 661 1581 or 800 232 0223
Facsimile: 703 661 1501 E-mail: styluspub@aol.com